I0103085

Vote ☐ YES or ☐ NO

Excuse me, can I see the third option?

Is YES a vote for business as usual?

Is No a vote of non-confidence?

Should an entire province pay for one city's transportation problems?

Is an inability to balance the budget an admission of incompetence?

Are we sick of lousy laws, poor services, exclusive contracts, executive salaries, bureaucratic bungling, benefits and bonuses all taken from our pockets?

Get real! City Hall belongs to citizens.

NO PAY WITHOUT SAY

Vote ☐ YES or ☐ NO

Excuse me, can I see the third option?

by

David K. Teertstra PhD

© 2015 Euclid Geometrics, Port Moody, BC

There are obvious problems in government, but citizens have no real say in their own institutions. Government workers also lack the power to repair what is broken. What a mess! Is the solution to pay even more tax? No. We need an enhanced democracy. Intelligent and caring Canadians must assert their right to act together to plot a sustainable course for our common future.

CIP

e-book ISBN 978-0-9686314-8-5

paperback ISBN 978-0-9686314-9-2

We Canadians have the creativity, intelligence and skill to make our country thrive. Freed from narrow job constraints and encouraged to innovate and improve our places of work, Canadians can cut obvious waste and strengthen our economy. But people must have a say in what impacts our individual lives and our common future.

All levels of government want more. Taking a larger slices of pie, what's left for you? You have no economic rights to protect your well-being. Wanting more means writing a law and using law enforcement to take their cut. Why is their inability to balance the budget not an admission of incompetence?

When was the last time your voice was heard? You have no say over major issues affecting your life. How about this: City Hall belongs to its citizens. All government belongs to its citizens. We created it. We are sick of being excluded.

We are sick of lousy laws, poor services, exclusive contracts, executive salaries, bureaucratic bungling, benefits and bonuses all taken from our pockets. We must have a say. We the people have the talent, the skill and the collective intelligence to balance the budget, set priorities and review all details of operations. We have the right: we paid for every pencil.

Vote Yes or No? Excuse me, is there a third option? How about this: include citizens in all details or we stop paying.

NO PAY WITHOUT SAY

HIGHER TAXES?

Can you imagine a country with a national highway allowing local bandits to toll each bridge? A few people are getting very rich by forcing everyone to deal with their complex toll system. The CEO of this toll system earns more than our Prime Minister. Is this public transit system run by civil servants, or is this a business taking massive profit from poor riders? Do taxpayers have any say?

Vote Yes or No, dear peasant, if you can manage to draw an X. Where is the third option that engages our intelligence?

Canadians already carry massive debt. Even a small interest rate increase places many in peril. Now an increased tax rate? We need some context – an overview in plain language as rough as hockey.

You are running like mad but not making it. You barely earn enough to break even. Now you have another system to attend to, a toll to consider on your daily drive, another password and account, threats of fines and consequences if you fail to pay attention. This is money and time taken directly from your children, from your life. 42% tax means 42% of your life spent serving government.

Vote Yes or No. Either way, you are voting for computers to replace human decision-making. If you thought someone with a clerk mentality was bad, computers are ruthlessly colder and more calculating. Computers do not care that you made a wrong turn or re-crossed the toll bridge because you forgot something. They do not care if you went bankrupt, lost your job, or if your best friend just died.

Did that red-light camera care that you slowed down to look for pedestrians? No. A ticket issued automatically engages you in a complex process beyond your control that costs too much to deal with. You give in and pay it. Or you don't give in ... but the system remains unchanged.

You sense injustice, but what exactly is the problem? Clerks and computers that cannot tell the difference between the intent of the law and the letter of the law. There is a big difference between the intent of public service (to build community) and business (to extract wealth). Voters worry that elected leaders tied too closely to big business are failing to act in the public interest.

Can our leaders only imagine economic growth based on population growth? If so, then immigration policy puts a million new people in the city - creating transportation problems and housing problems. If immigrants with wealth are favoured, then locals get bought out. As house prices inflate, banks profit and City Halls grow, but cities become unaffordable for Canadians.

The budget of City Hall was intentionally tied to house prices so that their growth did not exceed your growth. Capable of writing and enforcing laws, it is easy for any City Hall to act in self-interest and grow at your expense. As your house decays, government buildings rise. This is possible only if citizens are excluded from key decisions - such as land use policy.

Apparently, the idea is to put all businesses downtown and have no work available where people live. Let's be surprised by transportation problems. Let our leaders imagine just one solution: higher tax. We could make it favourable for some businesses to move out of downtown, but this reduces the tax base and works against the self-interested growth of City Hall.

Such major courses of action – legally skewed to favour a powerful minority and increase inequity - are ruining Canadian families and creating major problems of national security. We are generating a large population of youth with low-paid dead-end jobs facing a lifetime of debt with no hope of ever owing a home – who are locked out of the political discourse shaping our common future. Adding to this formula for disaster, scientists saying our country is on a crash course are silenced.

Canada has glaring problems, but your concerns do not impact policy. Here's an analogy. A normally maintained car produces a normal amount of pollution. A few obvious cars were major polluters, but we got a government system that forced exhaust testing on every normal car. It took decades to dismantle this mess, and now we are back where we started, unable to deal with the obvious polluters. Sensible people still have no say.

We have serious problems with transportation. Now our national highway has a toll bridge with automatic licence-plate readers and security scanners including high-resolution cameras with facial recognition. Government already has access to our phones, computers and finances. Instead using the national defense budget for this major military control point, they ask local taxpayers to pay the massive toll.

Vote Yes or No. Where's our third option, intelligent engagement? It is fearfully strange to have a democratic government resisting an improved democracy. Caring Canadians must have a significant say in our common future. Around the world, a few crazy people are running the show by muting the moderate majority.

Here's the deal. We are told that one in five people have mental health issues, and the unemployment rate is about seven percent, so obviously a significant percentage of government workers have mental health issues. Where is the evidence?

Any Canadian can cite a dozen examples of stupidity and injustice shoved down their throats by various levels of government. Here's a typical scenario overheard at a kitchen party. You pay tax when buying a home by borrowing money from a bank to meet the immediate needs of an inefficient government. You pay interest on that money for years after the government used it on short-term needs that included debt servicing. Think about it.

7

Here's another scenario. You pay taxes to City Hall (based on over-inflated house prices), but the gang there wants more and charges fees for services that you already paid taxes for. They even charge fees to file the form to register your business to pay taxes. They write bylaws that favour the growth of City Hall and then use the police to enforce laws that should never have favoured institutions over individuals to begin with. Was not City Hall was originally formed to serve the common needs of residents? Now we see perfectly good streets being repaved, conferences held and dinners served, fleets of new vehicles bought and shiny new buildings built as our homes decay. Nature is being paved under for ugly rental high-rises and there isn't a thing we can do about it.

To be clear, City Hall presents a sensitive face to your lack of empowerment. They let you design flags or comment on their plans and services, thus gathering ideas that they lack. But what you say has no real consequence: question the construction contracts and you'll be shut down real quick. Let's try this instead: City Hall belongs to citizens who have never abdicated their rights to approve the budget and modify all aspects of operations. Every dollar we pay in forms a legal contract for legitimate services.

We the people know how to run a tight household. We've learned how to be smart and lean in small business. We know how easy it is to spend other people's money, especially if the combined pool looks large. Does anyone in their right mind believe that a system of hard workers shackled to fast spenders can work? You want a tax hike? We want Citizens Oversight Groups to comb over and approve every detail of City budgets and operations. This is our garden and we have the right to pull weeds.

Not everyone believes big lies told on a vast scale. In Canada, we have "public corporations" claiming to belong to the public AND be legally separate bodies. Mediocre minds acting in self-interest have confused public service with business. They did so to rake in massive personal profit at public expense and avoid being held accountable. The public is shut out of the action and then accused of being disengaged.

Here's another reason people disengage with politics. Politicians said the tax hike was temporary, but it became permanent. It became harmonized, but not to your tune. Politicians promised and then broke the promise. But wait .... doesn't the Canada Revenue Agency (CRA) require us to report fraud? Does that mean lying or financial dishonesty? Maybe we should report fraud. Maybe we should tip them off about managers in Crown corporations giving themselves massive bonuses during a wage freeze.

Maybe we should report to the CRA that the CRA is encouraging unethical behaviour. Here is a group that wants a cut of every transaction. If you shovel your neighbors sidewalk, they want a piece of the action. But here's the rub: your elderly neighbor is on a fixed income and the City no longer clears sidewalks. Homeowners are responsible for that and the City just collects fines. You shovel your neighbor's walk and cut her grass because it is the right thing to do. It feels good. It provides a sense of belonging, a sense of home and place. It builds community and creates trust. It builds personal security and increases neighborhood safety. We must strongly oppose the ludicrous idea that society-building activities are financial transactions to be reported as an expense on one hand and an income on the other.

Here's a scenario. City Hall wants more money, and you understand rising costs. "Do you want neglected roads, do you want reduced services?" they ask, as if you were a child. But what they do not say, and what you may not realize, is that they are actually asking for a larger slice of the pie. With each level of government wanting more of your paycheck, what you get is less. Anyone can observe ridiculous expenditures and massive waste in government, plus people lining their pockets, but you the taxpayer has no say in the budget or operations. There's party going on and you're not invited. Does democracy consist of voting leaders in to run rampant a few years?

How about this instead: any claim by City Hall that they cannot balance the budget is an admission of incompetence. If government cannot balance the budget, we citizens will balance it for you. City Halls were created because a few people living in the same area found it economic to build and share a road - or to do a dump run, build an ice rink, share a power line. Citizens own City Hall. Listen up Mister Mayor: we handed you buildings and vehicles and everything you need down to the last pencil and now you want more? Now you plan to drive everyone into debt, so our money goes to debt servicing instead of services?

The fact is, individuals have no economic rights to protect them from the unhindered growth of each level of government. Downloaded fees, 42% total effective tax (according to a Fraser Institute report), interest payments to banks and increased costs of living leave you with little to build your life. After all these legally-enforced expenses, you find you cannot maintain your house. If you go bankrupt due to external economic impositions, then suddenly it's entirely your fault?

To be clear, a bank wrote you a note with no real value by borrowing from your neighbor at ten times leverage and is counting on your labour to provide that empty note with value. For every dollar you deposited, the bank leveraged other people into debt by a factor of five times to ten times to forty-two times, whatever they dared risk. Then they used an army of lawyers to craft one-way deals that say they win and you don't.

Life in Canada is designed like a circuit board. Yes, you have options. There are various paths to take, but all paths eventually lead to diodes. Diodes are electric devices that only allow events to happen in one direction. And that direction is not in your favour: it's one-way non-refundable.

You know the circuit well. Get a phone, get a job, open an account. Ding! Pay fees and taxes. Ding! Get a car. Ding! Get insurance. Ding! Get gas. Ding! Get food. Ding! Get TV and internet. Ding! Go out for a drink. Ding! Get a ticket. Ding! Get educated. Ding! Go shopping. Ding! Cross a bridge. Ding!

Your every move is a source of profit. Ever been to a hockey game in a big city? A lot of people are finding it's just not worth it. It's not just about the money - getting dinged for every move from parking to sitting - the game isn't what it used to be. There's something false here, over-calculated, systematically manipulated.

The fact is, you work hard for your money and think it has value because you can trade those notes for goods. Bankers do not think that way. In the world of banking and investing, money is just a concept, an idea, a mathematical statistical tool used to control and take what has true value - the land and its resources. Bank notes are backed by nothing but concepts of debt. Money is a tool to control you, the worker of the land, the serf. Here are better ideas:

The land and its resources belong to the people.

The common currency belongs to the people.

The government belongs to the people.

Are we disengaged voters? No, we've been shut out.

So the government wants more. No news there. Year after year, they go after teachers. Teachers know all about being under scrutiny. But the fact is, there are all sorts of government departments and programs that never get that kind of attention. How about the hopelessly convoluted public entity we call Canada Revenue with an apparently unlimited budget? Don't they deserve some scrutiny? We all know there's a lot to fix over there, starting with a website of links that lead to links that lead to links. And their tax system? Loopy! Mediocre minds create complexity.

If you search through the tens of thousands of government programs, you'll find all sorts that you could never have imagined could be running on your dime. And within each, all sorts of bungling ineptness that would never happen if it wasn't someone else's money they were spending. Taxpayers wanting better value take note: legally, each dollar paid in ties directly to an executive salary.

But at every turn, you pay without say. You pay without say. You must. Stop paying, even if you have good reason, and the full weight and mechanisms of the law will come down on you. But on what moral, ethical or logical principle? Is this what we call democracy?

We Canadians definitely need to talk about the law. It's a convoluted mess of old and new that could use a good renovation and clean-up. Most people are guided by an internal sense of right and wrong, largely learned in families, so some say that lack of knowledge of the law is no excuse for breaking it. If we are doing something wrong, we either know it for sure or kind of know it by a gut feeling. But some law must be learned: consider what you needed for your driver's license test. Some law is so complex that you need to be a lawyer, like business or tax law.

Other laws are non-intuitive, ill-conceived, misapplied, nearly impossible to grasp. They simply got passed at a moment in time by someone with an agenda who pushed it through. But there it is, ruining your life. You had no say when it was created and you have no say now. But there it is, applied with authoritarian force.

One of the problems with law is access to information. For example, you plan to cross the border and want to know in advance what the rules are. But you did not learn about and could not guess this one: a Canadian cannot drive a car with US plates in Canada. Is that a new law? An insurance problem? What is the purpose? The wise person does not ask a border agent these questions. They can seriously mess with you and seem to enjoy doing so. They have unlimited powers and you have no recourse. Instead, you are busted or bounced back to fix the problem - somehow - and it ruins your trip with resounding repercussions.

Later, you try to find out if such a law even exists. Was it a Catch-22? No, apparently the law does exist, and it has something to do with an unfair economic advantage. You don't even have a clue what that is or how it could work. Who wrote this law? Why? It probably has something to do with a general directive to make border crossing as difficult as possible. Canadians neither want nor need such ridiculously frustrating laws. And we really want to know (in the distant wake of a Free Trade Agreement) why prices remain so high here and so much less a short drive away.

Here is a truly unfair economic advantage: massive executive salaries taken directly from low-wage workers who know painfully well the real value of a dollar. These pocket-lining criminals have taken over our public institutions from transit to health care to car insurance. Higher taxes, rates and fees? No, we need those punks gone.

Canadians instilled with great pride in their country can get a rude awakening at their border. Our pride is diminished after observing how easy it is to emplace an authoritarian police state. Welcome to the modern world, bristling with technology but still desperately in need of people who really care. Humans can be nasty animals, whereas we really need to call out our virtues.

A comedian could imagine a public corporation with a provincial monopoly on auto insurance - writing a mission statement to become the leading insurance provider. They already are, enforced by law, so evidently we ought be proud to have provided jobs in upper-management for the mentally challenged.

After being forced to get rid of hundreds of managers with no one to manage, thus saving hundreds of millions, this public corporation imposes a double-digit rate increase on drivers. Their yearly report weaves spin and gloss and reads like a fantasy wonderland but is unbelievable because it lacks realistic grit and excludes known problems. Herein lies uninspired leadership and demoralized workers.

Perhaps we need clearly defined purposes and principles to hold our public institutions accountable. We need to fiercely defend peace and justice. As these are not businesses, we can start by removing the corporation status that protects inept CEOs and managers.

Do you still think you have a say? Now is the time to renew your dog license. City Hall wants money for your dog. But what is the problem they are trying to solve? What exactly do they do? Are licence fees siphoned off to other departments? Does this entity called City Hall care at all about dogs or have any expertise whatsoever? Stop paying until you get answers.

Our major problems of housing, labour and transportation that can be solved if government becomes opens to the talents and skills of all its citizens. People need to work together for the common good if we are to survive – we are ruining economies and ecosystems too quickly. We need to revise the rulebook.

Canada remains a land of law-abiding citizens who value peace and freedom. We are multicultural immigrants, aiming to respect other cultures and religions - but living on Native land. Historically, we watched a wretched and devastating civil war to our south and chose Confederation peacefully and slowly, by the pen and not the sword (but only after our own war and after England found the colony too costly to maintain). Of that we can be proud and we must continue on a peaceful course. But our world is changing rapidly (in ways not anticipated by the Constitution Act of 1982) and we need a strengthened democracy. No one wants our common future marred by politicians battling for provincial powers.

Working inclusively and thoughtfully, we need the talents and ideas of all caring Canadians to create a sustainable future. We need parents to sit with children to map it out. We need to work together, for everyone's sake.

THE BIGGER PICTURE

As a society, we progress by solving our problems. We improve by focusing on what is wrong. If this economy is working well for you, you may have a rosier picture than presented here and the following observations are not for you. This book is for everyone who has been dealt a short hand and painfully understands the need to drastically improve our country. A few people are running the show by muting the moderate majority and stealing your financial future. We have to speak up. We the people have the right to shape our future and shape it as we see fit.

Oxfam estimates that by 2016 the richest one percent will own more than half the world's wealth. The Canadian government is helping them succeed here. Canadians are being bought out, leveraged out, sold out. Financial giants are controlling our country, taking our resources, our businesses, our homes. We are being driven into permanent debt by the power-hungry few.

You can't earn enough to get ahead. Homes cost a fortune. You have no food rights. No privacy rights. No economic rights. You are shut out with no say.

Canadians love a rich political debate with friends over coffee or at a kitchen party, but only after the sports debate winds down. In Canada we have freedom of speech, but we also realize that many new immigrants come from oppressive regimes and are terrified to talk politics. If you say something significant - something everyone is thinking but won't say publically - would you suddenly be of interest to the Canada Revenue Agency? Would you suddenly be on the radar of Canada's spy network?

Consider that latter question. Those quiet mice want to know who everyone is, where they are now, what they are doing and saying, who they are talking to, how much money they have and what they are doing with it. Your driver's license photo was specifically taken for use in facial recognition software and there are cameras at every intersection. Automatic license-plate readers track your every move. Why do you need ID and a credit check to get a cellphone or computer that gives you no privacy?

You may imagine that Canada has not quietly emplaced a surveillance state, but if ever you have interacted with the police or crossed the border you quickly discover they have complete access to everything. Complete access is written into the contract you signed with Bell, or with Rogers, a mega-conglomerate controlling much of the media. We are right to be afraid.

We live in an age when the world's richest man owns a company that can turn your computer on in the middle of the night. Who else can do that?

In this age of computer hacking and spying, you must assume that anything written or emailed is scanned and anything significant said is recorded. This is the age of big data, data mining and metadata, and our Canadian spies are among the best in the world. You've been profiled and categorized. Do we want our government so closely tied to big businesses that only care about increasing profit?

If you write "The people of a country have natural inherent rights to self-determination," which is a foundational constitutional declaration and a cornerstone of democracy, then in some countries you could be killed. In Canada, a statement like that continues to make those in power nervous, particularly if the majority of Canadians locked out of the debate do not like the way things are going. In some countries, opposing voices are silenced by murder, prison or house arrest. In Canada, there are a dozen nicer social techniques to exclude and silence concerned citizens, including economic control. You are too busy drowning in debt to do anything substantial. You live in a bank-owned property but only you pay the property tax.

If you write "The resources of a country belong to the people of the country," then whoever thinks they own that cash cow will suddenly be very nervous. The fact is, no one asked for your opinion on Canada's energy future; quite to the contrary, your opinion is not welcome. You do not get to shape policy. You do not get to see the pipeline deal. The fact is, you are not asked about many things that affect your daily life, that affect your children's future, that affect the trajectory of sustainable life on this planet.

If you write "The common currency of a country belongs to the people of the country," is that statement not central to our inherent right to self-determination? Money is the main instrument of control in any country. With all your skills and talents, with all your hard work, why are you just not making it?

Who reading this has not been on the bad end of a deal with a bank? We need a better deal.

The terms of the Canadian deal have been dictated to us. After voting, how can we engagement with government? Letter-writing? Polite street protest? Unfair laws, downloaded fees, disproportionate taxes, convoluted systems, cash grabs, obvious injustice ... every individual complaint is stonewalled. What happens to your email? Control-delete. Isolated, you cannot know that ten thousand others complained about the same problem. Control-delete.

As individuals, we are required to demonstrate ethical and moral behaviour, but to be fair we must insist on reciprocity in business and government. Wait a moment ... ethical behaviour in business? Yes, if a business is systematically robbing you, we should call a thief a thief. Petty crime pales in comparison to corporate crime.

Just as no one is impressed with the ability of the RCMP to deal with corporate crime, so is no one impressed with the ability of our armed forces to buy or build ships and planes. What wrenches are clogging their gears? How can we help?

We have to talk about the economy. Is it really a house of cards? Nonsense: we all do solid work. The economy is actually an ecosystem. The problem is that the low-hanging fruit has been plundered. Never-ending exponential growth with profits funneling to a few is an unstable economic fantasy, a limited-time deal. This fantasy of never-ending riches is destroying our planet and your financial future. How on Earth are your children going to live? If you care about your kids, then fight for their future.

A stable economy, like a wheat field or orchard, is a beehive of healthy activity with flat-lined output. Zero growth, like your paycheck. We have to stop dealing with banks wrenching exponential growth from your flat-lined income. If there are wolves at your door, stop feeding them. The Romans called adding debt to debt the worst form of usery and so should we. We need a better deal.

On a vast scale, banks are behaving so badly that the world has been brought to the brink of financial disaster. European governments now need to bypass banks to get money to people who need it – quantitative easing – but are afraid to address fundamental problems including an incorrectly applied equation for exponential growth. This is your mortgage equation.

We need to talk about housing. How are your children ever going to afford a home? Can you? Which is more important: the market speculators profiting at everyone's expense, or you having a home? A generation ago, a home was a place to live, not a market. Now, the entire economy seems to hinge on housing. The rich are buying us out after using our labour to get rich. The few making big gains are making life miserable for the majority who just aren't making it. Here is the real winner: a large fraction of what you earn goes to banks. Here is the sick joke: they've used our money to leverage us into debt. Who are these jokers?

We have to talk about work. You have broad talents and deep skills, but are locked into a narrow job description. You have no real say outside your cubicle. You have ideas for improving things but are shut out of the action. And why help a company that quit caring long ago? Why indeed, when the profit is funneled out of the country? Is Canada being bought out to make us a country of wage slaves and renters? What do you think? Are you getting ahead?

Here's a picture for you. A child gets a paper route to earn money for Christmas presents. Gets up early on frosty mornings lugging heavy papers to your door before school. Proudly feeling adult, opens a first bank account. Christmas comes and its time to shop. But the bank teller tells the ten-year old "You owe us twenty-two sixty." Apparently there was a flyer with fine print about new rates and fees that put the account into overdraft for which there was a fine. Some slick language says they can do it to us whenever they like. Merry Christmas.

Listen, we have to call a thief a thief. If someone steals your cellphone, why is that a crime? Think about it. What effect does it have on you? Stop reading now and define the principle. What is it? If business or government is having that same effect on you based on that same principle, why are they not called thieves?

Why are they not held to the same ethical and moral standards as you? How exactly do you think the one-percent will own 50%? Through hard work? Get real! Now when you see a bank, think this: "I will not deal with criminal organizations."

Do you think that is harsh? Let's talk harsh. Do you know what a hospice is? End-of-life care. You can donate gently used goods to a hospice store run by volunteers who know the importance of end-of-life care. This significant societal and spiritual work also reduces health-care costs. Now what kind of monster taxes used goods in a hospice – goods that were already taxed when they were first sold? And why can't you do anything about it?

As each level of government increases its share of the pie, what remains for you to build your life? You have no economic rights. You have no say in their operations. As big business increasingly clamps down on basic human needs of food, clothing, shelter, transportation and communication, will you have any room left to breathe? As we increase the population of young people with crap jobs and no hope to ever own a home, increasingly policed and financially dinged at every turn, what do you think will happen?

Just the national economy is based on your personal economy, so is national security based on personal security.

Canadians deserve a better Canada. We must reshape our country. We have to, for everyone's sake.

STREETCORNER SNAPSHOTS

Imagine standing on a downtown street corner in your town or city. There may be a Petro Canada station, a Starbucks or Tim Hortons, a Royal Bank or Bank of Montreal, a London Drugs store, a Safeway. Perhaps you are a student looking for work, aiming to save for college or university. Problem is, you can never earn enough at any of these places to make it through the month, much less save for school. It costs too much to rent a room, too much to buy food. It costs too much for a phone, for transportation, for clothes. And if your parents support you, their earnings are actually subsidizing the company. Even with their support, you may not earn enough to save for school.

Lucky for you, the government is prepared to hand out student loans and credit card companies have special offers for first-year students. Four or five years later, there you are, graduated and standing on that same street corner looking at those same businesses that line every street across the country. Waving your shiny new degree, now you are more likely to get hired. Problem is, you still may not earn enough to meet monthly expenses and also pay off your student debt. A massive debt that keeps increasing through the magic of adding debt to debt.

Being young and optimistic, you are willing to work hard. You have drive and determination. You know you are going to make it. Four or five years later, if you are lucky, there you stand on that same street corner finally free of student debt. That freedom feels great. Now you can move ahead. But as you move ahead, every four or five years something major happens. A new job. A wedding. A baby. A move. An accident or illness. Divorce. A funeral. You continue to work hard, to excel, to grow and innovate, but something strange is going on. No matter what you do, no matter how hard you work, you simply cannot get ahead. After every four- or five-year period, you are no better off than before. Now you are 50 and still looking for that big break. Now you are 60 and realizing you can never retire.

The majority of Canadians now realize they are not getting ahead. Prices are rising but your paycheck isn't. It's like this. Imagine you have an apple orchard. To get that orchard, you worked hard to save a down payment and then borrowed a lot of money. You tend the trees all year, fighting frost, beetles and bugs. After each harvest you pay the bills and have little left. For years, you labour only to have someone else eat the fruits of your labour. How does this differ from indentured servitude? Is this the freedom your grandfather fought for? Are you brave enough to fight for your life?

Now you stand at your local street corner with a different perspective. What you see are systems. Systems designed to harness your labour, carefully crafted to funnel profits to a few. Across the street, a small group of people have seized control of a common natural resource, oil, to amass immense personal profit. Next door, a small group of people have seized control of the common currency, printing notes freely to leverage everyone into debt. Over there, another group has seized control of a basic human need, jacking up food prices for massive personal profit. Each of these groups knows how to profit from your every move. They employ armies of lawyers plus experts in statistics and human behaviour. Your life events may surprise you, but not them. They profit from your honesty, from your work ethics, from your talents and innovations, even from your ethical errors. They profit from peace and also from war. You, my friend, are a human resource, like a tree or a cow. If you don't like it, too bad. There are plenty of unemployed people ready to take your place.

Businesses proudly proclaim their mission to be the number one leading dominating ... whereas we want good products, good services, fairness and ethics. We care not a whit about your childish goals to be the next power-hungry Napoleon. Banks are quieter about their goals to seize 100% of your disposable income. They take the opposite control tactic: now you must bend over backward to prove your "credit rating", an indicator of how much more you can be taken for. By wearing suits to look legitimate and never saying "mark" or "sucker" out loud.

Systems are easy to create, emplace, maintain and enforce. A few people with good intentions can create a system for the common good, like public car insurance, but these systems are commonly hijacked by upper management wolves aiming to increase their personal wealth. A so-called "leader" seizes control using many tricks, but mainly this trick of psychology.

Growing up with parents in charge along with other authoritarian figures such as teachers, it seems natural to have leaders in charge of our organizations. But business leaders are different. Parents really care for their children, whereas organizational leaders could care less for you because they behave according to self-preservation. With a massive ego and a monstrous sense of entitlement, your money means little to them. It's so very easy to take and spend other people's money. Just set up a system.

Despots, dictators, czars, kings, queens, emperors, pharaohs, presidents, plutocrats ... we have a long history of "leaders". They are special. You are not. They have authority. You do not. Some leaders use swords and guns to enforce authority, while others claim to be gods or representatives of God, but most are good old-fashioned slavers. In the United States, individuals could amass great wealth using slaves. There is a basic business cost of slavery because slaves have basic human needs of food, clothing, shelter, transportation and communication. After slavery was outlawed, landowners used a peonage system wherein workers had little to no control over their conditions.

Today, those wishing to amass great wealth on the backs of others use diffuse business systems. If a business is defined as a separate corporate entity with several owners (principle shareholders plus investment groups), then no single person can be held responsible for wage-slave conditions. Especially not if everyone is doing it.

Take a moment to list the basic human needs of slaves. Then take a look at our Canadian Charter of Rights and Freedoms. Comparing the two, what rights are missing? Were they specifically excluded?

Peony? Wage slavery? This is rather fierce language to describe Canada. The typical Canadian is tougher than a snowstorm and inclined to celebrate our success stories. Canadians look to the bright side and are loathe to complain or speak negatively. We love to talk weather, sports and politics, but generally keep mum about religion or personal debt. Canadians speak freely about politics because freedom of speech is a Constitutional right and because our politicians realize they can operate almost independently of voiced opinions. Politicians may react to ten thousand voices shouting together – but only after estimating their chances of re-election – and only after estimating how they will gain. [The basic motivation is genetic, with self-preservation being fundamental to survival. Next comes group survival, keeping the department or organization alive and well. The problem occurs when their insatiable growth reduces your well-being, thus violating the purpose of the organization.]

When was the last time your complaint to a politician or company was taken seriously? All you get is control-delete. When ordinary people have no say in government, is their only option is polite street protest at officially designated locations? Around the world, small groups have seized control to force their limited agenda on the moderate majority. Do you think Canada is different? In Canada, they smile and wear suits. "How can I help you?" actually means "How can you help me?" The face is friendly and the slogans slick until you owe a nickel. Try getting your government to put people first and see what happens. We expect control-delete, but how about this: no pay without say. Higher taxes, tolls and fees? No pay without say.

Stop paying into systems that are ruining you. Form groups that stop paying. Tune in, turn on, drop out? No. Get engaged.

Canada functions only because many people work long hours and late nights for low pay with no benefits doing dirty dangerous dead end jobs they don't like. They do not complain about systematic unfairness or injustice because their voices will not be heard. They have obligations to family, are in inescapable debt and are busy fighting to keep their heads above water. Many major companies in Canada offer only these survival jobs. Survival jobs. Fighting to meet basic human needs. You may not like this language but it is descriptively accurate.

If you prefer truth over your comfortable image of Canada, then make a special trip to your local grocery store. Not for food, but to observe their organizational system. Notice the people. Most of the workers are young and there are a few overseers. Obviously, the store runs on a large number of low-wage workers. Ask one how much they earn. Ask if they earn enough to buy food from the store they work at. Ask if they earn enough for rent, or can save for school. But do not ask them if they will ever own a home because the answer is obvious. Speculators have driven the cost of a home far beyond reach. These people are fighting for basic human needs of food, clothing, shelter, transportation and communication. Later, on the internet, learn who owns the company and how much they earn. Then, consider the social trend. What do you think will happen as these massive wage disparities and economic inequities continue to polarize? What has always happened?

We humans have a great capacity to rationalize and make excuses. If you are a shareholder or a customer of one of these wage-slave companies, you are an embarrassing part of the problem. But how can you avoid systems designed to control daily life? You rationalize. Presumably these wage-workers have moral flaws and such low skill that they could not do more demanding and better-paid work. Perhaps, but you may be surprised by the knowledge base and complexity of rules required in this industry. And if pay increases with skill, intelligence and experience, as in a meritocracy, you would expect those at the top to be super-geniuses. One look at our political leaders in Question Period reveals they are not. Your boss at work is not a genius. Instead, the drive to minimize wages and maximize workloads is enforced by those at the top simply because they can get away with it. The owners are running large systems with a lot of inertia and clout. They have power and leverage and will do whatever it takes to keep it.

Consumers in Canada have little real choice. If you do not like one grocery store, you may have to travel far to another. How sad when you learn that these two stores are just two faces of the same company. Brand loyalty? What nonsense! Some giant holding company, along with a bank, has used their leverage to buy up grocery chains. What you thought was seven separate stores is actually a seven-headed monster. Does that matter when there are only a few major suppliers for all grocery stores? Everywhere you go, the game is to maximize food prices to maximize shareholder profit. The game is to minimize wages and benefits while maximizing workloads and productivity. Any company not doing this is at a competitive disadvantage and vulnerable to buy-out. They must do it if everyone is doing it.

[Although we like think our ourselves as independent conscious beings, we worry very much about what others think and exhibit as much group behaviour as any other mammal. There is individual survival and group survival. We know our collective group behaviour is changing the planet on a vast scale - and a thermodynamic law equates this change to irreversible degradation.]

What do you prefer? Rough but clear language, or the clever use of language to snare and entrap, to spin and manipulate? What will happen to the economy if everyone uses this business model: don't pay employees enough to be paying customers.

Anyone who started a business from scratch should profit. To start and run a business requires considerable risk. There are insurance and marketing costs, licenses, fees, taxes, accountants, lawyers. You pay for everything down to the last pencil. It's risky. By contrast, the wage of the hired help is guaranteed. However, the situation is different when a business becomes large and stable and goes after inescapable human needs. The management may take unrealistic incomes plus bonuses completely disconnected from any sense of equity or reality. The business could be going bankrupt and managers still refuse to ask employees for help or ideas.

Investors in mining have now grown wary of companies set up merely to take investment cash with no real hope of return on investment. The directors take your money because they can. And some tech companies with practically no sales are valued solely for their investment trajectory. Are we that desperate? That deluded?

Big business, aided by government, is doing well attempting to control every aspect of daily life. Once again: standing on your street corner, you are surrounded by cameras. Some are first-generation robots, automatically issuing tickets with ruthless efficiency. Your drivers licence photo was taken specifically to suit facial recognition software. That cell phone registered to you has a GPS system recording exactly where you are and who you are talking to, and the contract allows any level of government access this data. You could not prepay or pay-as-you-go, but instead underwent a credit check allowing full access to your finances. You have no choice - either agree or you don't get a phone. Want to complain? That cell-phone company is a seven-headed conglomerate that owns much of the media, from newspapers and magazines to radio and television – and they only report stories they can profit from. Control-delete.

Do you imagine you can catch a break by promoting your work, your invention, your new designs on the internet? That search engine company is in the business of gathering and selling information - the same as the spy business. No privacy on phone or internet? You're not worried. You've done nothing wrong. Quite to the contrary, it is YOU that is being systematically hacked and plundered. You are the Canadian cow, easily herded by the cowboys. Government and business have systems, but you, the isolated individual, do not.

Think about the word processing program you use. Why are we all paying for it over and over again when a few first-year computer science students could write another one in a summer?

Red-light cameras. By the time you get the ticket from this robot, you don't even remember where you were. If you do the right thing, a rear-mirror check, a look left and right for pedestrians, keep an eye on what other cars are doing, then in that split second the green can change to yellow. By then you are into the intersection and the yellow is short, too short. Is this about safety? No, there are other ways to warn you the light

34

ahead will turn red. No, this is business and government testing what they can get away with.

How about this: the GPS in your car knows what street you are on and automatically issues a ticket every time you exceed the speed limit. Every time you cross a bridge. Is that right? On what ethical principle do we put up with these ruthless robots? It's time to take them down.

Got a problem with a shoddy law in Canada? Good luck engaging with that! You'd have to put your whole life into it. Got a problem with a product? There's a 1-800 number that brings you to menu options. You may never get a live person, but if you do they simply re-explain company policy. Then you get a tit-for-tat series of one-liners with this low-wage call-center employee until it's clear you'll get nowhere. Good luck with a complex issue needing more than one sentence. You just got a pacifier stuck in your mouth. When was the last time you were asked? About anything? Did that change policy?

Business has now seized upon the basic human needs of food, clothing, shelter, transportation and communication to successfully put a continual squeeze on all Canadians. On a vast scale, they have eroded fundamental freedoms of self-determination and violated basic human rights. They do it for money. They do it because they can. They do it slowly and consistently, because they know sudden moves provoke sudden reactions. After too many complaints, we get unbelievable slick spin like "Oil Jobs. Greening Our Future." Suddenly scientists acting for the public good are enemies of the government and anyone caring about human health or life itself are eco-terrorists? By now, we have been conditioned to expect businesses to act without ethics or morals, but government too?

Historically, before Canada was Canada, this was a land of natural resources for France and England. Native opposition was either crushed or coerced into the fight between France and England for land and resources. England won, divided the spoils, and emplaced its systems of law, finance and ownership. Systems that are still with us, systems that define owners and serfs, the entitled one-percenter kingdom-builders and the rest of us. We maintain refugee camps for displaced Natives (pathetic little reserves) and people have no say over the use of "Crown" land. While living disrespectfully on native land, our great "Action Plan" is to ship more raw resources and weld pipes while wasting the talents of millions of Canadians with advanced degrees? How idiotic is that? We could have a resource economy plus an intelligent economy (like Japan, doing well with few natural resources).

In all this, businesses have not broken the law because Canadians lack fundamental Constitutional rights in key areas. Canadians have no rights to a clean and healthy environment. Canadians have no food rights. Canadians have no housing rights. Canadians have no economic rights. Canadians have no privacy rights. What other rights are missing?

For many people, from the poor to the middle class, Canada is an economic prison. At least in a real prison you get food, clothing and shelter, perhaps even TV, internet, an education and some form of a social life. For a single mother in a big city, Canada can be a hell-hole. You cannot improve your lot by moving to another city or province. What happens when the systems emplaced by business and government in Canada are inescapable? If a business becomes so big as to create an inescapable monopoly, must they also not bear broader social responsibilities?

At present, the legal articles of incorporation of companies allow them to act like big babies. They are in the give-me give-me me-mine stage of adolescence, only concerned with what they can get. That may be fine when a company is small because the consumer can choose whether or not to deal with them. Consider a small town with one grocer, one car dealer, one bank … in the absence of real competition these monopolies have you over a barrel. Standing on street corners that are the same everywhere, it is clear that Canada is small enough to be dominated by national and multinational companies. There's no real choice, especially when companies act in concert. Is it their way or the highway? No. Instead, we must insist that companies operating in Canada bear the full set of responsibilities required by a reasonable thinking adult. We must insist on changing the articles of incorporation.

Here's the thing about rights: you have to stand up for them. Here's the thing about fundamental rights: you have them regardless of whether or not they are written into a constitution. They are fundamental, inherent, intuitive, logical, scientific, moral, ethical. Here is an example. Food comes from the Earth. Plants go directly into our bodies; their molecules become our molecules. Food is essential to health, to life itself. Our food rights, our rights to know ingredients, our rights to a clean and natural environment, these are inherent and obvious. But companies have tampered with our food on a vast scale for profit and not for health. And we have no food rights. We need to act now to ensure food security.

Companies have tampered with food at the molecular level. They have altered DNA itself (inserting life-destroying chemicals into genes), but we have no way to observe changes at a molecular level. For a newly created chemical, there can be no evidence of a problem. Now attach a profit motive, and suddenly comes a claim that this chemical is safe! Consumers are test grounds for Frankenfood, but companies interested only in sales do not gather information from you, the sick consumer.

Canadians are sick and tired of one-way deals that always favour companies. We know that companies always want to increase profit at our expense. We know that upper management wolves want million-dollar bonuses and massive incentives. We know these companies quit caring decades ago. Sign the user agreement or get lost! We know the RCMP are unwilling or unable to prosecute such widespread corporate crime. Steal a chocolate bar and an entire system is prepared to prosecute you in perpetuity. Give yourself a thirty-million dollar bonus after ruining the company? Oh, you naughty boy! Perhaps ordinary people can no longer afford the ultra-rich.

This is what you may see at the grocery store: security cameras and a sign asking you to leave your backpack at the desk "for your safety". What a lie! Besides implying that customers are thieves, there is another obvious lie: simply look at the prices to discover who the real thief is. Does an extra dollar on each item increase the perceived quality? No, you are simply paying for someone's second mansion. It is the saddest thing ever to see retirees coming in daily hoping for some markdown bread.

We've all been burned. A common tactic is to use a partial truth, like red light-cameras "for your safety". If that were true, then all proceeds should go to the injured! We have parking meters that function only to address the cash problems of City Hall. We have trickily-placed fire hydrants as cash cows. Is this a real problem for firefighters? How about giving the proceeds to unemployed engineers to make a better system? Whoever wrote you that ticket had better have very good reasons for doing so. Are they simply abusing authority and applying leverage to take what they want?

City Hall has no incentive to kill these cash cows. They have no incentive to be tight and lean. They have violated their mandate to work in the public interest, but the trick here is to not make it too obvious: put on a good face and seek prey in debatable grey areas and shadows. Write unclear mandates and exclude significant public input.

Social and economic justice is a major problem we must deal with, but there another urgent and pressing problem. Humans are famously destructive. Humans will kill the last dodo or fish the last fish for profit, or destroy the land that is the basis of our existence. You may deny climate change, but can you deny this? Canadians wiped out great herds of bison, fished out the Great Lakes fisheries and destroyed the surrounding forests, chemically ruined our great St. Lawrence, plundered the Grand banks fisheries into a state of non-recovery, fenced and tilled under every possible scrap of prairie ... and now we are reaching the end of the fish in the oceans. We are driven to finish the job because the price increases for the last living whale, tuna, sea otter, walrus or elephant tusk.

These lost ecosystems that once were great drivers of the economy do not simply spring back to life. Why not? Well, each system has been degraded in ways we cannot fully comprehend. We know a physical law of thermodynamics describing how systems become irreversibly run down. Ruin it and there's no going back. Think you can work your spin around that?

Here's how a grocery store destroys the economy: they don't pay employees enough to be customers. If the wage-slaves run around scrapping for deals at other stores, then the grocery-system response is to reduce discounts and have fewer deals. The managers play poker: either you pay the highest possible price or we throw it out and lock the bin. But behind the food system are banks. Banks bleed every single person along the food chain, from the farm to the truck to the factory to the store to you. And at the end of the day, they've got you because you have to eat. But what about karma? What about all that ill will that got dished out? Do grocers and bankers really think those chickens aren't going to come home to roost?

Could consumers act together to care for everyone along our food chain? Could we cut prices by cutting out the waste stream going to compound interest? Can we collectively yank off those blood-sucking leaches?

Canadian consumers observe a steady decline of quality goods as companies produce more junk that breaks, falters and fails about the same time the warranty runs out. We hear legends of solid tools that slowly wore or never broke and could be repaired. Can you fix your own car? Now our manufactured factory food is crap, tampered with in every possible way for profit. We lack effective mechanisms to enforce honesty.

That's probably not tuna in the can.

Crab is the 20th ingredient in the crab cake.

Why can't you buy something made in Canada?

Have you accepted the fact you will never get out of debt?

Banks suck billions out of our economy - where does it go?

Could it be that our growth-based economic system is faltering because we are running out of Nature to exploit? Could it be that we will finally be forced to consider sustainability? Must we finally admit that our economy is based on Nature? That the world is finite?

Have you heard of the petri dish problem? Bacteria are placed in a small glass dish with food. There's plenty to eat, so the population doubles and doubles again. That's called exponential growth. With half the food left, that looks like a lot of room left for growth. But one half is one generation away from disaster. The end of the line. Backed into a corner with no options, the system will be permanently degraded.

When you borrowed money, did the debt-dealer warn you about the tipping point? Once you pass it, you will never come back. Thought you could beat the system? Many people enter a lifetime of inescapable debt – actual indentured servitude – or are permanently degraded, bankrupted by a system designed to do just that. What will happen when houses prices double again?

Do you know about black holes? Gravity gets stronger and stronger as you get closer. The force doubles, then doubles again in half the distance. Then there is something called the event

42

horizon. Cross that and there's no coming back. Not ever. And no one will ever know what happened to you.

Do you know about Higgs bosons? Apparently some particle out there is affecting all the other particles. We can't see this "God particle," but we know it exists by its effects. We only know about it because scientists put aside their individual interests to work together systematically. The Higgs acts just like an ultra-rich heavyweight, a person we never meet but that nevertheless affects everything we do. Just because a person has money does not give them the right to control your destiny.

This is what has happened to the housing market. Not so long ago, a carpenter could be married with four kids and pay off the house. Now, just a generation later, past the tipping point, past the event horizon, his carpenter son is a single renter with no hope of ever working on his own house.

Some people think that house prices will never crash. They cannot believe that house prices are just inflated paper balloons, puffed up by speculators that are controlled by the hidden Higgs-like heavyweights. They also never imagined that the price of oil would be instantly cut in half, and never even noticed that gas prices dropped by far less. They forgot the true wealth of their father's generation in the same way that no one alive in Toronto remembers how rich and productive the land once was. Like gamblers, homeowners look to a few winners and imagine they will win too, but real estate agents restrict access to the true numbers that include all the losers. Not realizing that the house odds are steeply stacked against them. Ignoring the human cost.

When you borrowed money, did you really think you could grow faster than the lending rate and also beat inflation? Did you borrow because you weren't making it? Now you've got the same bills as before, plus significant interest payments. The debt sellers aimed to get 100% of your disposable income and they did it. Even the tax you pay goes to debt servicing! Do you really think there are seven steps to financial freedom? Most likely, your financial advisor is getting rich. Most likely, you are on step one, seeking an income that exceeds basic expenses.

On a vast scale, our country imagines it can print money and spend its way out. Do you imagine you can continually borrow and spend your way out? No, if you find yourself stuck in a hole, it's best to stop digging. And if you find a leech on you leg, it's best to yank that bloodsucker off.

Consider our orchard again. An orchard teems with vibrant activity if everything stays healthy, but cannot possibly increase the number of apples produced year per acre. Now add to this balanced system the stupid human idea of continuous exponential growth. How can we extract more value every year? How can we get more money? The farmer knows this story well. The result of this incorrectly applied idea of exponential growth is to destroy the family farm. Decrease the quality. Dilute the product. Destroy nutrients. Add synthetic ingredients. Increase shelf life. Increase prices. Drive down wages. Import apples from elsewhere and increase our food dependency. Finally, replace the orchard with a condo complex, a bakery and a winery producing over-taxed zero-nutrient booze that you can drink on the curb where a productive orchard once was.

Our government has long ago stopped looking out for people. Apparently democracy consists of electing a few politicians to run rampant a few years. Some politicians run about the country busily thinking up sentences that sound important but lack significant content. Once elected, despite being devoid of ideas, they shut you out. Even if a politician originally aimed to work for public good, they discover themselves as cogs in a system controlled by big business. It is great sport poking fun at these hapless creatures, but do keep in mind that they often really do not know what to do about the major problems Canada faces. They also cannot gain traction without significant public support. There are some things that can only be done by groups of people using their collective intelligence to work for the common good.

Lacking input from the great pool of intelligent and caring Canadians, what is Canada's Action Plan? To cut more trees and pump and burn everything faster? To ship more raw materials for other countries to refine to sell back to us? Apparently we are not smart enough to refine tar sands or make products ourselves. Apparently we will all be welders on a pipeline, desperately trying to pay off houses we can't afford. Canadians suspect but have no idea how much money will be pipelined out of the country by that foreign energy giant. We are not privy to the details of the contract. We have no say.

Consider this ecosystem: Canada has a hardworking population of workers that are taxed to support a population who lives on that tax. Minimize wages and what happens to the tax base?

In a faltering world economy, Canada has become a safe place to stash your cash. If your country is failing, the obvious solution is to get your money into a stable country, financially backed by the hard work of Canadians. Did you make your money under a communist system? Did you make your money under a religious government? Under despotism or nepotism? By robbing your country's resources? No matter, all aboard! Skilled Canadians will eagerly work in your businesses and rent your apartment towers and offices. To the multinational corporation or global commodities group building those towers, Canada is a cash pipeline ripe for plunder. Complacent Canadians will put up with anything.

Consider this: anyone with enough money could buy all the homes and businesses in a small country. Maybe their investments could "help" Haiti. Everyone could be permanent low-wage renters with their basic needs met. They could be free to work at the sewing factory or the shoe factory, to live in the north or the south. But lacking the true freedom of economic self-determination, those Haitians would also be peons. Do you think this is an imaginary scenario? Do you have any idea where your clothes came from?

Are you getting the picture? You are part of an ecosystem. A Canadian fashion designer is linked to a clothing manufacturer large enough to be listed on the stock exchange. You buy the clothes and also participate in the stock market either by choice or by investments that are forced on you by the Canada Revenue Agency. Your money in someone else's account for someone else's use, the sooner the better.

Consider the clothes you wear. You may imagine that deplorable conditions in overseas sweatshops are eased by non-profit organizations, but the CRA shackles the income of non-profits. Non-profit workers attempting to improve society end up standing on street corners begging for change like hobos because they are not allowed to make and sell books or videos depicting the deplorable conditions in overseas sweatshops.

Apparently we should not use the word hobos. No offense intended. Maybe we should invent nicer language like "employment insurance" which makes no sense. Maybe we should be less direct and call a corporate thief an innocent opportunist because they are after all wearing a nice suit completely at odds with our image of a thief.

Listen up, you language police: dig deeper into the basis of morality. Maybe we like Clint Eastwood when he says "Get off my lawn, punk." Perhaps we prefer straight-shooting over the annoying coyness of Parliament's Question Period that makes intelligent adults look like petty children. Maybe we wearisome of Republicans hating Democrats so much that they'd rather destroy the country than help people.

The overall message from any economically-controlled government is "Don't let anything interfere with business! There are too many factors you don't understand." Those in charge are nervous nellies, saying "Don't touch it! Don't change anything! It's going to get better, you'll see. If only we do this ... or this ... or this." What nonsense. Infinite growth? Get real! An economy based on the fantasy of unlimited exponential growth is a house of cards. Forced growth is the economic mechanism by which we are leveraged out of what truly matters: the land and its resources. You life is leveraged. Why work with no gain?

When citizens work together to split the cost of shared services (e.g. roads, electricity, water, waste collection), this saves money, builds community and strengthens the country. If the road-builder is local, the money stays in the community. Businesses do not have goals of strengthening society; they aim only to maximize profit and increase personal wealth. What do you think will happen if we continually privatize public services? What right does a multinational company have to drain money out of our country?

At one moment in time, in a backroom meeting you were not invited to, a few people made a major deal that suited them and decided your future. We were leveraged out of work we could do ourselves. It is in the interest of citizens to work together.

The truth is that every single Canadian has a broad range of skills and talents, inventiveness and ingenuity, physical skill and intellectual prowess. Unleash our potential and we'll do well. Give employees the power to fix obvious problems and our institutions will run better. The problem is that everyone is locked into a narrow job description, treated like peon sheeples and told to shut up and work. And we have to, to make ends meet, to get that good reference. Increasing complexity and responsibility is added to our job description and eventually each of us is asked to do the work of two! The job descriptions posted by companies are now unbelievable. To get hired, people now make remarkable claims on resumes that are equally unbelievable.

The problem is that each Canadian as an isolated individual is on lock-down and their ideas for improving life fall on deaf ears and echo off institutional walls. What ever happened to individuals before institutions? What ever happened to personal security as the foundation of national security? True security comes from knowing your neighbors and caring for people, and definitely not from increased surveillance and harsher policing.

The sad fact is that Canadians are shut out of the national conversation and not free to improve their own country. We have the terms dictated to us via carefully worded political monologues on topics of no great import or relevance. But unleash our skills and talents and we as a people can thrive.

WORK, WORK, WORK

Consider the sad fact that many talented Canadians want work but cannot find it. Job-seeking from home, recrafting resumes to suit corporate slots, months go by, then years. Many work part-time jobs without benefits. Many work full-time but really want meaning beyond making rich company owners richer. We want work with purpose, fulfillment and recognition. We want work that builds lives and communities. We want great national projects that we can participate in and be proud of.

Being unemployed doesn't do a lot for your pride. Many people would rather get a small stipend working for a positive cause than receive government assistance and be forced into another inept program. Although this is your city, and across the street is City Hall with a ton of work that needs doing ... these two never connect. Although this is your country, and there is a lot Canada could do with that huge unemployed labour force to build the country... but ... nothing.

Face it, we know people will be unemployed at times. Some need improved skills, training or experience. Can we not envision a nation-building work program? We could build trails, campgrounds, shelters, improve parks and wild-lands. We could repair the homes of the elderly, make a national website about Canada, solve problems of homelessness, fix banking, improve our aging infrastructure and so on. The fact is, life on a reserve or in a small town can be a crashing bore and then kids get into trouble. If you are young, dispossessed and disengaged with no outlet and hope for a future, isn't this a recipe for radicalization? Building our country could be the experience of a lifetime, a reason for national pride.

Instead of admitting that for many Canadians the economic recession is almost as bad as the 1930s dustbowl, Canadian policymakers project an image of Canada as a recession-proof miracle. The fact is, our banks were just as bad as American banks in the race to the bottom when it came to writing mortgages. It's just that our bailout was quietly tucked away into the CMHC by spreading the burden on everyone. Regardless, would it not improve the image of Canada to care for its most desperate people? Have we no pride?

Why does City Hall exclude citizens? They've signed business contracts and are locked in. We the people need to unlock our own resources, open up the place and get to work. Are we not strong and free? Do you feel strong and free?

51

Although City Hall belongs to citizens, a few people have seized control of it for personal gain. This is not democracy, but an idea imported from the old social structure of Britain in which mayors and lords controlled and oversaw their property - the workers of their land. This is kingdom building. But if a small group in City Hall has seized power, writing nonsensical, amoral and unethical laws to favour their growth, then the only solution is for citizens to assert their democratic ownership. With people excluded, it is "the government" not "our government". We the people must be in charge of approving the budget and operations.

Similarly, our universities are traps for students. A university requires plenty of work to function, but that work is contracted out and not available to students. Instead, students are targets for companies, cash cows for industry, fresh meat for the debt sellers. Teachers and professors feeding on tax dollars failed to fight to make schools a place where students can focus on studies.

Instead, some smart-ass MBA working for a bank thought they could make money by leveraging students into debt. As business and government cut students out of significant work, and as everyone jacked up the rent, are we suddenly surprised by student-loan default rates? Instead of admitting to crimes committed against students, provincial governments instead vote to never forgive student debt. Not ever. In this economic prison you have no right to work off your debt. This government demands money but refuses to supply jobs.

Politicians complain that voters are not engaged with the issues. The truth is that our leaders cut us out of the important action. Here is a prime example. Everyone who has ever dealt with the Canada Revenue Agency knows about their massive inefficiencies and problems. We send and receive all sorts of mail. We go through loops of calculations that we know will be irrelevant. We are never told about significant deductions. We closed our business operations years ago but cannot get the CRA to listen. We know they have cumbersome antiquated systems and people who are expert at doing nothing but looking busy. We know there are highly-paid managers with no one to manage. But does the government allow us to improve the system or make it fairer? No. Instead of fixing problems within the CRA, year after year they go after the budget of teachers. Is it not shocking to you that the Minister of Education is not fighting for education? It is up to us to fight for a fair tax system.

Here is another example of government cutting you out of the action: public auto insurance. Overall, it's a pretty good system but one that does not survive close scrutiny. Here is a human scenario. Someone poor Joe needs a car to get to a distant job with marginal pay. Every dollar counts. They are forced by law to engage with this system, but in it are managers with incredible pay and benefits giving themselves massive bonuses. Next, our poor Joe has a minor accident and the insurance company resists paying. Specifically, the time and expense required to make a claim is onerous and barely worth it. What is this nonsense about a deductible amount? It simply means that someone has spent the money you set aside for an emergency. That poor person would have been better off putting their monthly payment into an account that these insurance scoundrels had no access to.

The idea behind insurance is to create a pool of money because at some time one of us will have an accident. The idea is that we care for one another. But some scoundrel in charge cannot resist finding a hundred excuses to spend your money, including creating an entire department to deny claims. Clearly, we do not want public insurance to be used as a cash cow to make individuals rich or to feed other parts of government. The fact that you put money in substantiates the contractual requirement that your money is to be safeguarded and used only as intended. But that fundamental contract has been broken, the foundational principles of insurance have been violated, and you have been shut out. Does that make you angry? Get past anger and move on to resolve. We need morals, ethics and minds as sharp as swords to clean up this mess. We need engagement, not exclusion.

Similarly, if a business has become so large as to monopolize common needs, or if businesses act together to control, drain and debilitate society, your rights to the common good must be asserted forcefully. Our current Constitution was created by politicians in a top-down manner, whereas the people of a country maintain inherent rights to self-determination.

Our Constitution Act of 1982 was created at a time when computers were not in widespread use. Now, systems are being rapidly emplaced to automate decisions affecting all details of your life in Canada from health care to auto insurance. But the motive is profit and not public good. Our leaders have not mapped out a sustainable future.

Computer systems can be designed to use many people to enrich a few. Consider the artist or inventor who labours hard to create and invent and then wishes to be known and rewarded for their hard work. They create a website or video to connect with the world. But on the other side lies a company seeking ideas. Why should a company hire you when they can simply download your work and use it disguised with a twist and a fresh coat of paint? They call it big data or data mining. To be clear, any company doing data mining is not especially interested in whether you bought Kelloggs or Nabisco. They are mining for the nuggets of gold, the inspired ideas or work that took years to create, the ideas that will make them big bucks, the ideas they can take without a paper trail.

Consider the plight of a poor manager who exaggerated their skill set. They don't know what to do. Haven't got a clue. So they post a job posting and ask all the candidates to describe what they would do. They fill file folders with other people's ideas. They ask employees how they would improve things and then claim that work as their own. In this system, job hunters are ripped off and employees asked to hand over their best ideas for nothing. This is the nature of corporate theft, with bloodsucking vampires seeking prey in the legal grey areas and shadows.

Is it your dream to shape your life to suit company requirements? Is it your dream to build something so you can be bought out? Should corporate articles of incorporation exclude acting for societal good?

Is the system working well for you? Statistics Canada spins the opinion that Canadians are doing better than ever, but even the net worth of the top 20% of income earners (accumulated over a lifetime, including inheritances) remains less than half the cost of a house in a major city. Is this what we call doing well? The fact is, it does not cost that much to build a house. Houses are not worth half a million: this price tag is simply speculation. Many groups and individuals seek to profit from rising prices, from property owners to City Hall to banks. Banks are the biggest winners because compound interest makes owners pay for their properties two to three times over. By the time the mortgage is done, you have a thirty-year-old tear-down.

With house prices so high, what will your children do? With wages stagnated, they will never own a home. Or, never pay it off. To make it, they must move far away form their parents, tearing families apart. How do you think this system will evolve? Specifically, incomes are flat through time but banks demand ever-increasing profit. This is false growth, designed to put people down. Like our orchard, the only possible outcome is general degradation of human life as the rich to get richer. Using our labour, the rich then buy up our businesses, factories and homes to generate a nation of low-wage workers and renters.

This is not speculation. This is what is happening. Everyone imagines they are a big-shot wheeler-dealer, wanting an investment property to generate rental income. Apparently the renter will earn enough to pay the mortgage plus expenses, but not enough to buy their own place. But in reality the renter will not care for the place as if it were their own and you will have considerable work and expenses as a landlord. It may not be worth it.

What if you don't want your life to be on the open market?

Over a generation ago, homes were not an investment. Homes were places to live and people had savings. They had the cash leverage to start a business. Now, the entire economy is degraded and hinged on the housing market. Entire countries are banking on the basic human fight for shelter. Old people now count on selling their home as a retirement plan because they have no cash and no savings. Investors now see the elderly as their next get-rich plan. Listen up, you punk: get away from my grandmother.

In all of this, we have an ever-increasing population of youth without hope to ever have a decent job, without hope to ever own a home. We have an increasingly disengaged disenfranchised people who have been shut out of government, shut out of business and whose voices are not heard above the drums of the rich pounding more, more, more! More? To what end? To consume every bit of land, to crowd out Nature to extinction, to blacken the skies and melt the ice caps?

Is this cynicism or simply a description of our societal trajectory?

Cronyism. Capitalism. Socialism. Marxism. Fascism. Most of us could care less about the "ism" labels. We simply want the freedom to live fairly and enjoy life, to fulfill our goals and dreams, perhaps not to be rich but at least to be happy. We want homes and children and a good meal. We really really really don't want war. We certainly do not want someone telling us what to do, especially if that person wants you dead for not believing what they believe. We don't want a small group of nasty folk with guns and religious excuses destroying everything we've worked for. We don't want financial overlords controlling our every move for profit, and we don't want to be taxed to death. We don't want a surveillance state controlled by computer programs and robots. We can handle personal freedom and personal security and the responsibilities that come with it.

Can Canadians renovate their own country? Those in power will immediately say no because the system is working well for them. But the fact is that we have worked in your offices. We know the systems. We've seen all the tricks, including the year-end budget burns to make sure you get more next year. We've seen the make-work projects. We've seen good clean simple working systems replaced by hopeless hapless high-maintenance complexity. We know how people specialize in looking busy while doing nothing. We've seen good people squeezed out of organizations by power-hungry sociopaths uncomfortable with truth and honesty, intelligence and integrity.

Canadians have the right to renovate government because it's our government. Canada belongs to its citizens who maintain an inherent right to determine our future.

Canadians are already acting together, just not consciously. Our group behaviour is polluting skies, killing fish, putting plastics into the ecosystem, generating junk food, driving up costs and generally making things worse for the next generation. We Canadians must act together to plot a survival course, a course that could also create a sustainable economy. Can we craft ethical banks and modify business life to suit us?

What issues matter most to you?

Can we rank the top ten issues?

Can we do a series of projects to improve life in Canada?

Can we demonstrate the positive power of democracy?

Can the voices of the moderate majority be heard?

CANADIANS, SHAPING CANADA

Now is the time for action: we must take back City Hall. We also need a broader plan: we Canadians must shape our common future as we see fit. Parents must sit with children to define and shape the future of our country. The Constitution of a democratic country expresses the will of the people. It is our prime directive stating our intentions, inspirations and aspirations. As the laws of a country arise from the ethics, morals and sense of justice of its people, higher ideals must guide our institutions. As a people with natural and inherent rights to self-determination, what kind of country do we want? Let's start the discussion.

Our Constitution Act of 1982 including the Canadian Charter of Rights and Freedoms was written by political leaders in the best interests of the people despite difficult federal and provincial power struggles (see Canada's Constitutional Revolution by Barry L. Strayer, 2013, University of Alberta Press). The Constitution, written to be accessible, understandable and applicable to the grit of our daily lives, is now the top guiding law of our land. But it was not written by the people for the people and excludes many common-sense rights critical to daily life.

Much has changed since 1982. It was hard to imagine global economic strife, widespread pollution, global warming, collapsing ecosystems. Fundamental changes to the makeup of food now directly affect the security of the person. Today, personal debt loads and unaffordable housing allow societal peonage and institutionalized wage slavery that severely restricts individual rights to self-determination. We need to get rid of rules that don't allow us to do the right thing.

The common use of computers, necessary tools now indistinguishable from cellphones, allow education and communication and also unprecedented levels of spying and corporate information-gathering. Creative works of individuals that drive and sustain the economy are now easily mined by big business. Concerned Canadians can list many such problems, some more pressing than others, that we may systematically solve by a strengthened Constitutional Act. We could create a national website wherein the collective intelligence of caring Canadians can be voiced.

If we were not fearful of political correctness, would we ask more interesting questions? Could we take a poll? What would you ask? How many Canadians feel that government became mean-spirited this past decade? How many Canadians want a limit on the time a political leader can be in power?

Our law is quite effective in dealing with injuries inflicted by one person on another because direct cause and effect may be demonstrated. Institutionalized abuse is a thornier problem. This is a worldwide problem in which a few individuals gain sufficient wealth, power and resources to set the agenda for the majority. At the root of the problem, our individual rights to self-determination are eroded as government and big business increasingly controls basic human needs beginning with food, shelter and clothing.

Canadians fought and died to protect our freedoms and continue to do so. The need to formally define and defend fundamental human rights arose after World War Two and directly informed our Canadian Human Rights Act and our Charter of Rights and Freedoms. Earlier, a peaceful Confederation was specifically sought to avoid the devastating civil war being observed in the states. We chose the pen and not the sword and must continue to do so. We Canadians will not have the terms dictated to us by a greedy power-hungry minority.

Our current concern is with diffuse social systems that intrude on all details of our daily lives and have the net effect of damaging the environmental basis of life. Diffuse means that a provable link is difficult to establish between damage to your life and the actions of a corporate or government entity. Individual lives see significant negative impact, and we sense some violation of our basic rights, but the specific source is obscure. We may be concerned with inescapable monopolies controlling every facet of daily life. Is our government unwilling or incapable of dealing with corporate crime, collapsed ecosystems and pollution?

Our institutions and corporations commonly present a complex web of rules and regulations without defining fundamental guiding principles. Were such laws written for the good of the people or for the benefit of the institutions and corporations? How can Canadians encountering unfair laws effect positive change?

One way to deal with diffuse and complex social systems is to systematically define our direction as a society. Our Constitution is a set of guiding laws representing the central principles directing Canadian society. It is the fabric of who we are as a people, defining who we aspire to be. We begin by describing the existing fabric.

Each of us encounters many entities in business and government, and each entity is a living organism seeking to survive and grow. Each entity emplaces systems of laws, rules and regulations, fees and taxes, to which you are subject by force of law. An individual must work to meet their basic needs but is then legally bound to feed these many entities. An individual, not making substantial gains, increasingly mired into debt by systematic forces and observing many entities acquiring incredible resources, may wonder for whom are they working. Is this ecosystem healthy, balanced or sustainable?

To address this problem, consider your survival an individual. You need air to breathe, food to eat. Water, preferably fresh and clean. Clothing and shelter for protection from weather. Look at the land around you and consider how materials provided freely by Nature are used to meet your basic needs. Elements from the Earth and molecules from plants built your body. Now consider the main industries providing food, water, roads, concrete and construction materials. These represent the economy basis that can be evaluated financially.

We must consider the human use of human beings as well as our use of land and animals. Should we double our population yet again and consequently remove the rights of wild animals to exist? Are people human resources like trees serving only to satisfy the purposes of a powerful few? Do not your talents and capacity as a human far exceed the corporate job description?

The scientific basis for the claim that the people of a country have inherent rights to the land and its resources is chemical analysis proving beyond the shadow of a doubt that our bodies are physically constructed of the materials of the Earth. An incredible web of life supports plants, and the molecules that form the plants are digested by us animals to form our bodies. A reasonable person would lawfully conclude that we have significant inherent rights concerning both the environment and the food taken into our bodies.

Most criminal law is based on scientific proof of cause and effect. However, corporate crime and government corruption that negatively impacts numerous individuals and degrades the environment remains difficult to prosecute. Our social response could be to require that all corporations doing business in Canada behave like reasonable persons. Businesses and corporations must grow up and consider the external impacts of their actions; they must behave as reasonable adults sensitive to our most pressing social problems. All persons must be equal under the law, including a corporate entity defined as a person.

We need to talk about money. Money forms the fabric of a country. The common currency belongs to the people. Although a printed note is inherently worthless (as true value lies in the land, its people, its resources), the exchange of money is the substantial basis of a legal contract. On what ethical basis do we allow for-profit corporations to print notes backed only by their capacity to leverage Canadians into debt? Publically traded banks use fractional reserve banking for the sole purpose of making money (literally) while driving down wages. Their clever use of language and complex mathematics does not interest Canadians who become ensnared in inescapable debt only to funnel incredible wealth to a small group of individuals. Perhaps ordinary Canadians can no longer afford to support individuals with the power to enforce their ideology of unlimited power and wealth.

We need to talk about the mathematics of money. All financial and economy discussions are currently based on an equation for unlimited exponential growth, even though such growth is unrealistic, unsustainable and destructive. Here's how the math works. Out on a walk, your child asks you to carry a small pebble. That's not too much to ask, so you do it. As you get another and another, the number of pebbles doubles and doubles again. If the compounded weight eventually becomes too much to bear, the parent must say no. So it is with debt. Lenders have assessed human behaviour in great detail and know that we tolerate gradual changes but react to sudden events. As the cumulative effects of bad economic policy increasingly crushes Canadians, we get heavier policing and enhanced surveillance.

We need to talk about natural growth. Consider that the production capacity of an orchard, field or forest is limited and linear in time. Only so many apples per year. Now to the farmer we apply an economic model of exponential increase, who must then cut more, burn more, reduce quality, create corporate megafarms. Is the correct model? No. Any reasonable person recognizes that naturally sustainable ecosystems cannot exponentially increase production. Applying the wrong model wreaks environmental devastation. A poor economic model of unlimited exponential growth that funnels wealth and power to a select few has brought the world to the brink of economic collapse. Perhaps we need a sustainable ecosystem model.

We need to talk about loans and mortgages. An equation for unlimited exponential growth is being applied to your income which is limited and linear in time. An equation allowing debt accumulation is economically unsustainable usery. It is a mathematical certainty of compounded interest that land and homes, factories and offices must become unaffordable (valued far beyond construction costs). Government land use policies act to drive up real estate prices because their income is based on real estate valuations. People must work harder to provide the printed currency with real value. Is it now impossible to reap the rewards of your labour or to profit from the work of your own hands? To address unaffordable housing, consider that the people of a country own its land and resources. Crown land is our land and may be used to protect basic human rights that include affordable housing.

It is commonly asserted that the economy is driven by uncontrollable and mysterious forces. Nonsense. What we see in Canada is a broadly enforced economic policy to extract and export raw natural resources. We need not know the details of international deals to export oil or gas to know that great profits will go to a select few while pipeline workers will not be able to pay off their homes. We have a great education system allowing us to invent, develop, manufacture and export refined and developed products - but instead of getting cash to our makers and doers we set them up for exploitation.

We need personal financial rights. Economic rights. Environmental rights written into the Constitution and enforced by law. We must discuss energy, sustainability, rights to privacy and personal security. What matters to you?

We need to talk about jobs. Most of us work at jobs we hate, getting nowhere to make someone else rich. Most of us are in a narrow slot of a job description that contrasts sharply with our broad skills and expertise, creativity and talents. We have a vast pool of problem-solving abilities that could bring great wealth to this nation but we are stifled by pyramidal power structures within business and government. Is there a better structure for a richer human experience?

Looking around your community, there is much to be done. Look also at the unemployed and underemployed, or those with special talents. Connect those that need work to the work that needs to be done. Why do so many laws, rules and regulations stand in the way of obvious beneficial solutions? We the people need the legal capacity to put into effect our solutions to serious social problems. We need a Constitution written by the people for the people. We need a sustainable future.

We the people must have the right to improve the health of our government entities. Our insurance systems have forgotten that their primary purpose is to care for the injured. To do that, they must protect and not waste the pooled money. We all understand human nature when it comes to a collected pile of money. If paying into a system is enforced by law, then we create a cash flow system ripe for mismanagement. We see managers voting themselves raises and bonuses while the working poor struggle to make payments. We see inefficient unfair systems emplacing rules that serve the entity instead of the public. In order to prevent corporate crime, the public must be able to shape and control our public institutions, in particular those universal and inescapable entities employing force of law. Our citizens have considerable skill and expertise to vastly improve our public systems.

As children and parents, workers and scholars across this country consider our new Constitution, know that the best of us get bogged down in details and definitions and get distracted by irrelevant arguments and misinformation. As individuals in our Canadian cultural mosaic, each of us must rely on our own experience but eventually unite in a common vision. This great exercise, whatever its outcome, must not become a provincial power struggle or platform for special interest groups.

In a world of despots and dictators, armed rebels and self-declared rulers, Canadians can demonstrate leadership by peacefully effecting significant positive societal change. This exercise is not about imposing yet another a system on a population but is about living in a country of friends and neighbors with families and children and bills to pay. This is about mapping our way together into an uncertain future.

The 1982 Constitution including The Canadian Charter of Rights and Freedoms may be modified using a by-the-people for-the-people consensus to express the fundamental ideas and goals guiding our democratic society. As the guiding law of our land, our Charter inspires and provides our prime directives. It should provide powerful protection of individual rights and liberties, reasonably limited by our impact on others. Our elected government must again become concerned with the health and well-being of its citizens and their fundamental rights to food, clothing, shelter, privacy, transportation and communication. The laws of a country must reflect our ethical and moral constitution as human beings and naturally include logic, reason and scientific proof.

In an age of Wikipedia, when millions can instantly vote for their favourite singers and dancers, why do Canadians lack a platform for our voices to be heard? What do you think?

Considering what you observe around you, do you feel:

Proud?   Vote ☐ Yes or ☐ No.

Strong?   Vote ☐ Yes or ☐ No.

Free?   Vote ☐ Yes or ☐ No.

The results may surprise.

Best Regards,

David K. Teertstra

Writing from Port Moody, British Columbia, Canada in the spring of 2015.

About the author

This is not about the author. This is about you. But if you must know, Dr. Teertstra is an independent research scientist who developed an optical scanner for use in industry and medicine to identify materials, determine composition and probe molecular structure. PhD University of Manitoba.

Declaration of Canadian Rights

The world has changed. So must our Constitution.

The Canadian people maintain inherent rights to self-determination. The land, its resources and the common currency belong to the people. Canadians can reshape our national destiny as we see fit.

Economic Rights Our common currency must not be used to leverage Canadians into inescapable debt, to systematically control or leverage assets or to institutionalize societal peonage. Except to sustain society, no government or corporate entity may exert inescapable control over basic human needs including food, water, clothing, shelter, transportation and communication.

Environmental and Food Rights Our bodies form from food, air and water. Canadians have inherent rights to full knowledge and control of all aspects of the food chain.

Privacy Rights Our every move and action can now be tracked, monitored and used against us for power and profit. We have the rights to privacy and personal security.

We the people reserve the right to shape our common future.

www.ingramcontent.com/pod-product-compliance
Lightning Source LLC
Chambersburg PA
CBHW071233290326
41931CB00037B/2900